The Angel Cookbook

Heavenly Light Cuisine

by
Diane Pfeifer

Illustrations by Clark Taylor
Published by Strawberry Patch, Atlanta, Georgia

ISBN: 0-9618306-6-2
Library of Congress Number: 94-092351

Published by: Strawberry Patch
                  P.O. Box 52404
                  Atlanta, GA 30355-0404
                  404/261-2197

Editors: Gail Poulton and Diane Pfeifer
Design & Composition: Paula Chance, Diva Designs, Atlanta, GA

*To God for inspiring me in the City of Angels
and to my sweet angels,
Jeff and Jennica*

A tip of the halo to:
Dot, Gil and Leigh Ann for encouraging my kooky ideas
Mara Reid Rogers for food trivia
Gib Carson gang for spreading our wings
Sathya Sai Baba center for spiritual recipe testing

Table of Contents

Hollywood Halos

And The Angels Sing

Angel

Angel And The Badman

Angel In My Pocket

Angel Island

Angel Of Broadway

Angel On My Shoulder

Angels And The Outlaws

Angels In Disguise

Angels In The Outfield

Angels Over Broadway

Angels With Broken Wings

Angels With Dirty Faces

For Heaven's Sake

Going My Way

Heaven Can Wait

Heaven Help Us

Heaven Knows Mr. Allison

Heaven On A Picket Fence

Heaven On Earth

Heaven Only Knows

Heaven With A Barbed Wire Fence

Heaven's Gate

Heavenly Bodies

Heavens Above

Here Comes Mr. Jordan

It's A Wonderful Life

The Heavenly Kid

The Trouble With Angels

Wing And A Prayer

Winged Victory

Wings

Heavenly Harmony

A Star Fell Out Of Heaven

Angel Baby

Angel Gabriel

Angel In Disguise

Angel In Your Arms

Angel Of The Morning

Angel's Tears

Angel Flying Too Close To The Ground

Angels We Have Heard On High

Borrowed Angel

Earth Angel

Got A Date With An Angel

Hark The Herald Angels Sing

Heaven Knows

Heaven Must Be Missin' An Angel

Heaven Must Have Sent You

Heaven On Earth

Heaven's Just A Sin Away

I'm In Heaven When I See You Smile (Diane)

Johnny Angel

Kiss An Angel Good Morning

Knockin' On Heaven's Door

My Blue Heaven

My Special Angel

On The Wings Of Love

One More Angel In Heaven

Pennies From Heaven

Seventh Heaven

Somebody Up There Likes Me

Thank Heaven For Little Girls

Too Much Heaven

Saintly Starters

Holy Guacamole

Uto-Pitas

Paradise Pâté

Saintly Cilantro Salsa

Tortilla Halos

Heaven Only Nachos

Shep-Herb Mushrooms

Will the Kernel Be Unbroken

Artichoke Harps

Harmonious Hummus

Eggplant Cavi-Arch Angel

Guardian Garlic

Holy Guacamole

Makes about 3 cups

3 ripe avocados, peeled and seeded
1/4 cup chopped green onion tops
2 tablespoons fresh lemon juice
3-4 cloves garlic, pressed
1 medium tomato, diced
Jalapeño pepper to taste, seeded and finely chopped
1/2 cup chopped cilantro
Salt to taste
Chili powder to taste
Tortilla chips for dipping

In medium bowl, roughly mash avocado with a fork or wire whisk. Stir in remaining ingredients except tortilla chips. Let sit 15 minutes or longer. Serve with tortilla chips.

Uto-Pitas

Serving Size Varies

Whole wheat pitas
(large size for lunch, small size for parties)

Filling Options:

Diced avocado

Sliced ripe olives

Shredded Jack cheese (lowfat ok)

Chopped green chilies

Thinly sliced tomatoes

Alfalfa sprouts

Cucumbers, peeled and thinly sliced

Romaine lettuce, washed, dried and torn

Herb marinade (see page 50)

Cut pitas in half. Stuff each half with desired ingredients. Drizzle filling with small amount of marinade.

Paradise Pâté

Serves 16-20

1 tablespoon olive oil
1 cup chopped onion or scallions
1 stalk celery, chopped
16 ounces mushrooms, sliced
1-1/2 teaspoons dried basil
1 cup walnuts
1/4 teaspoon salt
1/4 teaspoon black pepper
8 ounces regular cream cheese, softened
2 teaspoons lemon juice

Topping:

8 ounces cream cheese (lowfat ok), softened

Topping Options:

Almonds, walnuts, sliced olives, parsley, red bell pepper pieces, etc.

Preheat oven to 350°F. Sauté onion, celery and mushrooms in oil until soft. Transfer mixture to food processor or blender and blend. Add remaining ingredients except those for topping. Blend until mixture is smooth.

Spoon pâté into oiled 9x5-inch loaf pan. Bake for 1 hour or until toothpick inserted in center comes out clean. Let pâté cool in pan for several hours, then refrigerate until firm. To serve, loosen edges with knife. Invert onto serving platter, tapping bottom of pan. Reshape if necessary.

Beat cream cheese until smooth. Spread layer of cream cheese over pâté. Create design with topping options. Serve with crackers or raw veggies.

Saintly Cilantro Salsa

Makes about 4 cups

1 6-ounce can black olives, drained
2 14-1/2-ounce cans peeled tomato wedges with juice
1 4-ounce can chopped green chilies or more to taste
4 green onion tops, chopped
1 tablespoon olive oil
2 tablespoons vinegar or lemon juice
2 cloves garlic, pressed
Salt and pepper to taste
1/2 cup chopped cilantro
Tortilla chips for dipping

In food processor or blender, pulse olives and tomatoes just until chopped. Place in mixing bowl and stir in remaining ingredients except chips. Chill for a few hours or overnight. Serve with tortilla chips.

Tortilla Halos

Makes 60-70

16 ounces cream cheese (lowfat ok), softened
2 tablespoons chopped green onion
1/2 cup chopped black olives
2 tablespoons chopped fresh dill or cilantro, optional
8 large-sized flour tortillas
Salsa for dipping

In food processor or mixing bowl, blend or beat cream cheese until creamy. Stir in onion, black olives and optional herbs. Spread thin layer of mixture on tortilla. Tightly roll up tortilla. Wrap individually in plastic wrap.

Refrigerate at least 3 hours or overnight. To serve, remove wrap and cut into 3/4-inch slices. Serve with salsa.

Heaven Only Nachos

Serves 6-8

1-1/2 cups grated cheddar cheese (lowfat ok)
Taco seasoning mix to taste
Tortilla chips
1 9-ounce can no-lard bean dip
Prepared guacamole dip (see page 12)
16 ounces sour cream (lowfat ok)
Jalapeño peppers, seeded and thinly sliced

Melt cheese in medium saucepan over low heat. Stir in taco seasoning and mix thoroughly. Spread tortilla chips with small amount of bean dip and cheese mixture.

If softer nacho is desired, microwave or broil until softened. Top with small amounts of guacamole dip and sour cream. Garnish with sliced jalapeños.

Shep-Herb Mushrooms

Serves 6-8

8 ounces fresh mushrooms

2 tablespoons margarine (lowfat ok)

2 tablespoons green onion, finely chopped

2 teaspoons fresh parsley, chopped

1 clove garlic, pressed

1/2 teaspoon salt

Pepper to taste

1 cup herb stuffing mix

1/2 cup boiling water

Wash mushrooms. Remove and save stems. Put caps in shallow baking dish. Heat margarine in medium pan. Finely chop stems and sauté with onion until soft.

Add parsley, garlic, salt and pepper. Cook for 1 minute. Stir in stuffing mix and hot water to make a stiff mixture. Stuff each cap and bake at 350°F for 15 minutes.

Will the Kernel Be Unbroken

Makes about 9 cups

8 cups popped popcorn
1 cup crumbled tortilla or corn chips, optional
3 tablespoons margarine (lowfat ok)
1 tablespoon taco seasoning mix or to taste
1/2 cup grated cheddar cheese (lowfat ok), optional

Place popcorn and chips, if desired, in large bowl. Melt margarine in small pan over low heat. Stir in taco mix and remove from heat. Dribble over popcorn. Toss with hands to coat thoroughly. Serve immediately or continue for a cheesy treat.

Spread popcorn mixture on greased baking sheet and sprinkle with cheese. Place under broiler until cheese melts, about 1 minute. Check constantly to be sure popcorn is not burning. Remove and cool before serving.

Artichoke Harps

Makes about 3 cups

1 14-ounce can artichoke hearts, drained
1 cup mayonnaise (lowfat ok)
1 cup grated Parmesan cheese
1/2 teaspoon garlic powder or to taste
1/8 teaspoon cayenne pepper or to taste

Preheat oven to 350°F. With spoon, mash artichokes in large bowl. Stir in mayonnaise, Parmesan cheese, garlic powder and cayenne pepper, mixing well. Place in buttered 1-quart casserole. Bake uncovered for 20 minutes. Serve with Melba toast, crackers or veggie sticks.

Harmonious Hummus

Makes about 2 cups

6 tablespoons fresh lemon juice
3/4 cup tahini (sesame paste)
3 cloves garlic, pressed
2 tablespoons soy sauce
Cayenne pepper to taste
1 15-ounce can chickpeas, drained, liquid reserved
1/4 cup chopped parsley

In blender or food processor, blend lemon juice, tahini, garlic, soy sauce, cayenne and 1/4 cup chickpea liquid until smooth. Add chickpeas, blending to a rough consistency.

If smoother or thinner texture is desired, add more chickpea liquid and blend accordingly. Stir in parsley. Serve with raw veggie sticks or crackers, or use as a sandwich filling.

Eggplant Cavi-Arch Angel

Makes about 2 cups

1 medium eggplant
3/4 cup tahini (sesame paste)
4 cloves garlic, peeled
1 teaspoon salt
5 tablespoons fresh lemon juice
1/2 teaspoon cumin
Paprika
Finely chopped parsley

Puncture eggplant with knife and place in baking dish. Broil 4 inches from flame for 20 minutes. Turn occasionally. Remove and allow to cool. Peel off skin.

In blender or food processor, blend tahini, garlic, salt, lemon juice and cumin until smooth. Add eggplant and blend again. Place in serving bowl and sprinkle lightly with paprika. Garnish with parsley.

Guardian Garlic

Serves 4

4 medium bulbs garlic
or
2 bulbs elephant garlic
Olive oil
Freshly ground black pepper
Choice of dried herbs: basil, thyme, tarragon, etc.
Narrow crusty French bread, sliced 1/2-inch thick

Trim bottom of bulb so it sits flat. Remove some of papery outer layers, leaving bulbs intact. Trim tops of cloves. Drizzle tops with olive oil and sprinkle with pepper and choice of herbs. Wrap each in aluminum foil.

Place on baking sheet or in baking dish. Bake at 350°F for 30 minutes or more until cloves are soft. Test with a toothpick.

To serve, squeeze garlic clove onto bread.

Garden of Eatin'

Sanctimony Macaroni

Ba-salvation Salad

O Come Lettuce Adore Him

Ro-maine-gel

Sub-Lima Salad

Endive Wings

Last Judge-Mint Tabouli

Cupid Cucumber Cooler

Lime Cilantro Salad Blessing

Bless-a-Me Sesame

I-Dill-ic Dressing

Thy Kingdom Kumquat

Sanctimony Macaroni
Serves 10-12

2 cups snow peas, stems and strings removed
2 cups cherry tomatoes, halved
2 cups mushrooms, sliced
1 4-1/2-ounce can chopped ripe olives, drained
1 16-ounce package elbow macaroni, cooked and drained
5 tablespoons grated Parmesan cheese
1 8-ounce bottle Italian dressing (lowfat ok)

In medium saucepan, place snow peas in boiling water. Boil for 2 minutes. Rinse in cold water and drain. Place in large bowl. Toss with tomatoes, mushrooms and olives. Stir in pasta, cheese and salad dressing. Chill and serve.

Ba-salvation

Serves 4

1 ball fresh unsalted mozzarella cheese packed in water*
2 large beefsteak tomatoes, sliced
1 bunch fresh basil leaves, chopped

Dressing:

3 tablespoons balsamic vinegar (no substitutions)
1 tablespoon Dijon mustard
1 tablespoon honey
1 tablespoon lemon juice
1/2 cup virgin olive oil
Salt and freshly ground pepper to taste

Cut fresh mozzarella into 1/4-inch slices. In oval casserole, stagger layers of mozzarella, tomato slices and basil. Mix dressing ingredients thoroughly. Pour over salad and refrigerate for at least one hour to blend flavors.

*Available at farmers' markets, gourmet deli shops and Italian markets.

FETA GREEK SALAD

O Come Lettuce Adore Him

Serves 6

1 small cucumber, peeled and thinly sliced
1 small green bell pepper, seeded and cut into strips
2 large tomatoes, diced
1 small red onion, thinly sliced
1/2 cup salty Greek black olives
Herb marinade to taste (see page 50)
1 head romaine lettuce, washed, dried and torn
6 ounces feta cheese, crumbled
Oregano, fresh chopped or dried

Combine first 5 ingredients in large bowl. Toss with herb marinade to coat. Arrange lettuce leaves on platter and top with salad mixture. Sprinkle top with feta cheese and lightly with oregano. Serve at once.

Ro-maine-gel

Serves 4

1 head romaine lettuce, washed and dried

2 tablespoons lemon juice

3 tablespoons olive oil

Salt and freshly ground pepper to taste

Dash garlic powder

Grated Parmesan cheese

Croutons

Tear lettuce into small pieces and place in large serving bowl. In small bowl, blend lemon juice, oil, salt, pepper and garlic powder. Toss into salad and top each serving with Parmesan cheese and croutons.

Sub-Lima Salad

Serves 6

2 15-ounce cans lima beans, well drained

2 teaspoons paprika

1 clove garlic, pressed

2 tablespoons olive oil

2 tablespoons lemon juice

Salt, pepper and cayenne to taste

1 teaspoon dried dill

3 tablespoons chopped cilantro or parsley

1 tablespoon capers, optional

Mix all ingredients together in large bowl. Marinate for at least an hour before serving.

Endive Wings

Serves 4-6

1 small head Belgian endive, washed and dried

Dressing:

3 cloves garlic, pressed

Juice of 1 lemon

1/4 cup olive oil

1/2 teaspoon ground black pepper

1 egg yolk

1/2 cup grated Parmesan cheese

Dash of Worcestershire sauce without anchovies

Salt to taste

Separate endive into spears and arrange in circular pattern on platter. In food processor or blender, blend dressing ingredients until creamy. Place in small dipping bowl in center of platter for a unique salad or appetizer.

Last Judge~Mint Tabouli

Serves 6

2 cups boiling water
1 teaspoon salt
1 cup bulghur (cracked) wheat
1 cup minced parsley or cilantro
2 tablespoons fresh chopped mint
1/2 cup minced green onion tops
1/4 cup olive oil
Juice of 2 lemons
Salt and pepper to taste
1 cup chopped tomatoes, optional

Pour boiling salted water over bulghur in medium bowl. Let sit at least 30 minutes to absorb water. Drain off any remaining water. Toss remaining ingredients into the wheat. Stir, mixing thoroughly. If desired, chill before serving.

CUCUMBER YOGURT RELISH

Cupid Cucumber Cooler

Makes 2-3 cups

1 cucumber, peeled and chopped
2 tablespoons chopped green onion tops
1 cup plain yogurt (lowfat ok)
Squeeze of lemon juice
Salt and freshly ground pepper to taste
2 tablespoons chopped cilantro leaves
Dash cumin, optional
1 tablespoon capers, optional

In medium bowl, mix all desired ingredients together.

Lime Cilantro Salad Blessing

Makes 1/2 cup

2 tablespoons fresh lime juice
2 tablespoons honey
3 tablespoons fresh cilantro
2 teaspoons fresh or 1/2 teaspoon dried basil
1/4 teaspoon cumin
Dash salt
1 clove garlic, pressed
1/4 cup balsamic vinegar
2 teaspoons olive oil, optional

Mix all ingredients in bowl. Let sit for one hour to enhance flavor.

Bless-a-me Sesame

Makes about 2 cups

1 cup tahini (sesame paste)
1/2 cup lemon juice
1/4 cup olive oil
2-3 tablespoons tamari or soy sauce
1/2 teaspoon black pepper
1/4 cup chopped green onion
1-2 large cloves garlic, pressed
Dash cayenne, turmeric and salt, if needed

In food processor or blender, blend all ingredients together until smooth. Let sit at least an hour or overnight to blend flavors and thicken mixture. Thin with a little water if needed.

AVOCADO DILL DRESSING

J-Dill-ic Dressing

Makes about 1 cup

1 ripe avocado, peeled and seeded

1 clove garlic, pressed

1/4 cup water

1 tablespoon olive oil

2 tablespoons sour cream or mayonnaise (lowfat ok)

1 tablespoon fresh or 1 teaspoon dried dill

Pinch sugar

1/2 teaspoon salt or to taste

2 tablespoons fresh lemon juice

In food processor or blender, blend all ingredients until creamy. Use for salads or as a dip for raw veggies.

Thy Kingdom Kumquat

Serves 6

Dressing:

2 tablespoons balsamic vinegar

2 teaspoons Dijon mustard

2 teaspoons soy sauce

1 clove garlic, pressed

1/2 teaspoon minced fresh ginger

1/2 teaspoon sugar

2 tablespoons olive or other oil

Salad:

3 small heads baby bok choy, well rinsed

Sliced kumquats

Combine dressing ingredients in small bowl. Set aside.

Cut bok choy in half lengthwise. Arrange in large microwave casserole. Add 3 tablespoons water. Cover and microwave on high for 2-3 minutes until stems are translucent and soft when pierced. Immerse in cold water until cool. Drain well.

Arrange in single layer in shallow serving dish. Pour dressing over bok choy. Garnish with kumquats.

Crocks of Ages

Holy Watercress

A-Maize-ing Grace

Serene Bean Soup

Lentils We Have Stirred on High

Pearly Gates-pacho

Heaven-Leek Soup

Chard-ian Angel Soup

Heaven For-Bisque

Split Peace-ful Soup

Peace-o Miso Soup

Clergy Curry Mix

Hollan-Grace Sauce

Cherubic Chutney

Miracle Marinade

Holy Watercress

Serves 4

2 tablespoons margarine (lowfat ok)
1 large yellow onion, finely chopped
1-1/2 cups potatoes, peeled and diced
1 bay leaf
4 cups vegetable bouillon broth
Salt and freshly ground pepper to taste
2 bunches watercress, washed
Sour cream (lowfat ok)
Dash paprika

Heat margarine in large soup pot. Sauté onion over medium heat until translucent. Add potatoes, bay leaf, broth, salt and pepper. Bring to a boil, then cover and simmer until potatoes are tender, about 15-20 minutes.

Discard tough stems and yellow leaves from watercress. Reserve a few sprigs for garnish. Chop the rest and add to soup. Cook for 2 minutes.

Allow soup to cool slightly, then purée in a blender. For warm soup, reheat for a few minutes and garnish as below. For cold soup, allow to cool completely, then chill.

Serve with a swirl of sour cream and watercress sprigs. Sprinkle with paprika.

A-Maize-ing Grace

Serves 4-6

1 large potato, peeled and diced
2 bay leaves
2 teaspoons cumin
2 cups water
1 small yellow onion, chopped
1 2-ounce jar diced pimientos
2 tablespoons margarine (lowfat ok)
3 tablespoons flour
1-1/4 cups milk (lowfat ok)
1 16-1/2-ounce can corn, drained
1 cup grated cheddar cheese (lowfat ok)
Salt and pepper to taste

In large soup pot, cook potato, bay leaves and cumin in boiling water about 15 minutes. In separate pan, sauté onion and pimientos in margarine until tender. Blend in flour. Remove from heat and gradually add milk, stirring constantly.

Stir milk mixture and corn into potato mixture. Simmer for 5 minutes. Remove bay leaves. Add cheese and stir until it melts. Season with salt and pepper.

BLACK BEAN SOUP

Serene Bean Soup

Serves 6-8

2 tablespoons olive oil

1 medium yellow onion, chopped

1 medium green bell pepper, seeded and chopped

4 large cloves garlic, pressed

2 cups water

1 tablespoon dry onion bouillon

2 teaspoons ground cumin

2 teaspoons ground oregano

1-1/2 tablespoons red wine vinegar

3 15-ounce cans black beans, drained

In large soup pot, heat oil over medium heat. Add onion, green pepper and garlic. Cook until onion is translucent. Stir in remaining ingredients. Cover and reduce heat to simmer. Cook 30-45 minutes.

Lentils We Have Stirred on High

Serves 4-6

2 tablespoons margarine (lowfat ok)
1/2 small yellow onion, chopped
5 cloves garlic, pressed
1/2 teaspoon grated fresh ginger root
Dash cayenne pepper
1 4-ounce can chopped green chilies
1 cup red or yellow lentils
4-5 cups water
1 slice lemon
Salt to taste
1/4 cup cilantro leaves, chopped

Melt margarine in medium saucepan over low heat. Sauté onion, garlic, ginger, cayenne and green chilies. Cover and cook for 5 minutes. Add lentils, 4 cups water and lemon slice. Season with salt.

Cook for 20-30 minutes until lentils have thickened. Add extra water for thinner texture. Remove lemon slice. Stir in chopped cilantro and serve.

Pearly Gates-pacho

Makes about 7 cups

1 28-ounce can peeled tomatoes with juice, chopped

3/4 cup chopped green bell pepper

1/2 cup chopped onion

1/2 cup diced cucumber

3 cloves garlic, pressed

2 cups onion bouillon broth

1/2 cup lemon juice

1/4 cup olive oil

1 tablespoon paprika

1 teaspoon salt

Black pepper, freshly ground

Tabasco sauce or cayenne pepper to taste

Chopped parsley or cilantro

1/2 cup toasted croutons, optional

In large mixing bowl, combine all ingredients except croutons. Chill for 2 hours before serving. Garnish with croutons, if desired.

Heaven-Leek Soup

Serves 6

3 large leeks, ends trimmed
2 tablespoons margarine (lowfat ok)
1 medium yellow onion, finely chopped
1 cup sliced mushrooms
3 large white or baking potatoes, peeled and diced
1 bay leaf
2-3 cups vegetable bouillon broth
1 cup milk (lowfat ok)
Salt and freshly ground pepper to taste
2 tablespoons chopped fresh parsley or cilantro

Slice leeks thinly, using white and palest green parts only. Heat margarine in large soup pot. Sauté leeks, onions and mushrooms over medium heat until onion is translucent. Add potatoes, bay leaf and just enough broth to cover. Bring to a boil, then cover and simmer until potatoes are tender, about 15-20 minutes.

With a spoon, mash some of the potatoes against the side of the pan. Add milk and simmer over low heat for 20 minutes. Season with salt and pepper. Stir in parsley or cilantro.

SAVORY SWISS CHARD SOUP

Chard-ian Angel Soup

Serves 6

2 tablespoons olive oil
1 bunch green onions, finely chopped
1 16-ounce can peeled tomatoes, puréed
1 16-ounce can cooked white beans with liquid
1/2 cup long-grain white or brown rice
4 cups vegetable bouillon broth
1 teaspoon dried or 2 tablespoons fresh, chopped basil
2 garlic cloves, pressed
Salt and pepper to taste
1/2 pound fresh Swiss chard leaves, washed and chopped

Heat olive oil in large soup pot over medium heat. Add onions and sauté about 1 minute. Add remaining ingredients except Swiss chard. Bring to boil.

Reduce heat to low and cover. Simmer about 10 minutes, stirring occasionally. Add Swiss chard and simmer another 5-10 minutes.

Heaven For-Bisque

Serves 4-6

1 tablespoon olive oil

1 large onion, chopped

2 cloves garlic, pressed

2 teaspoons ground coriander

2 teaspoons curry mix (see page 48)

1/2 teaspoon ground cumin

1 pound sweet potatoes, peeled and cubed

4 cups vegetable bouillon broth

Plain lowfat yogurt

Heat oil in large saucepan over medium heat. Sauté onion and garlic until onion is translucent. Stir in spices and cook about 30 seconds.

Add potatoes and broth. Bring to a boil, then cover and simmer about 20 minutes until potatoes are tender.

Transfer mixture, half at a time to food processor or blender. Blend until smooth. Return to pan and cook until hot. Top each serving with dollop of yogurt.

Split Peace-ful

Serves 6

1 cup dried split peas
1 bay leaf
3 cups water
1 tablespoon olive or other oil
1 teaspoon each dried basil, marjoram and oregano
1/2 cup chopped onion
1/2 cup chopped carrot
1/2 cup chopped celery
1 tablespoon lemon juice
1-1/2 cups vegetable bouillon broth
1 14-ounce can plum tomatoes, chopped with liquid
Salt and pepper to taste
Cilantro leaves for garnish, optional

In large saucepan, combine peas, bay leaf and water. Bring to boil, then reduce heat and simmer until peas are tender, about 1 hour. Drain and remove bay leaf.

In medium saucepan, heat oil over medium heat. Add herbs and cook about 30 seconds. Add onion, carrots and celery. Cook for 3 minutes. Add lemon juice, cooked peas, broth, tomatoes, salt and pepper. Cover and cook 10 minutes.

Transfer half of mixture to food processor or blender. Blend until smooth. Return mixture to pan and stir. Heat through and serve immediately or chill. Garnish with cilantro, if desired.

Taste test guaranteed by two picky five-year olds.

ASIAN MISO SOUP

Peace-o Miso

Serves 4

4 cups water
3-4 tablespoons miso* (any kind)
1 pound tofu, cut into cubes
2 scallions, thinly sliced
1 teaspoon sesame oil, optional

In medium saucepan, boil water. Stir in miso to taste until dissolved. Add tofu and simmer for 2-3 minutes. Stir in scallions and sesame oil. Serve promptly.

*Miso is a fermented soybean paste that lends a rich, soy sauce flavor to soups and dressings. It can be found in Asian markets, health food stores and the international section of many grocery stores.

Clergy Curry Mix

Makes about 6 tablespoons

2 tablespoons ground coriander
2 tablespoons ground cumin
2 teaspoons ground cardamom
2 teaspoons ground cinnamon
1 teaspoon ground cloves
1 teaspoon ground nutmeg
1 teaspoon ground turmeric
1/2 teaspoon cayenne pepper
1 teaspoon freshly ground pepper

Combine all ingredients in a small bowl. Stir well. Store in airtight jar. Use to season vegetables, sauces and soups.

Hollan-Grace Sauce

Makes 1-1/2 cups

2-1/2 tablespoons margarine (lowfat ok)
1/4 cup flour
3/4 cup milk (lowfat ok)
1/2 cup mayonnaise (lowfat ok)
2 tablespoons lemon juice
Dash salt

In heavy saucepan, melt margarine over low heat. Slowly stir in flour. Add milk, stirring constantly until thick. Remove from heat. Add mayonnaise, lemon juice and salt. Stir well.

Cherubic Chutney

Makes about 1 cup

1 tablespoon fresh ginger root, grated
1/2-1 teaspoon hot green chilies, minced
1 heaping teaspoon sugar
3 tablespoons cashews
Juice of 2 lemons
1/2 teaspoon ground caraway seeds
Salt to taste
2 cups cilantro leaves

Place all ingredients except cilantro in food processor or blender. Blend until smooth. Slowly add handfuls of cilantro and continue blending until chutney is smooth. Add small amounts of any ingredient until desired flavor is achieved. Let sit 2 hours or overnight to enhance flavor.

– 49 –

Miracle Marinade

Makes one cup

1/4 cup olive oil
1/2 cup red wine or balsamic vinegar
1 teaspoon Dijon mustard
2 teaspoons mixed dried herbs
(Herb choices: basil, tarragon, oregano, thyme, marjoram, dill)
Salt and freshly ground pepper to taste
2 cloves garlic, pressed

Combine all ingredients in a jar with a tight-fitting lid. Shake well. Let sit 1 to 2 hours before using. Refrigerate and use within two weeks.

From the Other Side

Devout Sprouts

Goodwill Dill Potatoes

Black-Eyed Peace

A Wing and A Pear

Homily Hominy

Gos-Summer Squash

Glorious-paragus

Tidings of Comfort and Bok Joy

Joyful and Try Eggplant

Para-Diced Vegetables

Mir-a-Kale Polenta

Blissotto Risotto

LEMON BRUSSELS SPROUTS
Devout Sprouts

Serves 4-6

1 pound Brussels sprouts
2 tablespoons margarine (lowfat ok)
Juice of 1/2 lemon
Toasted pine nuts
Salt and freshly ground pepper to taste

Trim and wash sprouts. Halve lengthwise. Steam or microwave until barely tender. Melt margarine in large skillet. Toss in sprouts and cook until heated through.

Add lemon juice, pine nuts, salt and pepper. Toss before serving.

POTATOES WITH DILL
Goodwill Dill Potatoes

Serves 4

3 large white potatoes, peeled and chopped
1 green onion, finely chopped
1 teaspoon dried dill
4 tablespoons grated Parmesan cheese

Steam or microwave potatoes until tender. In medium mixing bowl, beat until creamy. Stir in onion and dill. Spread evenly on greased baking sheet. Sprinkle with cheese and bake at 400°F until browned, about 10-15 minutes. Cut into equal servings and remove with spatula.

Black-Eyed Peace

Makes about 4 cups

1 14-1/2-ounce can peeled tomatoes with juice, puréed
1 16-ounce can black-eyed peas
1 4-ounce can chopped green chilies
1/2 medium yellow onion, finely chopped
Juice of 1 lemon
3 cloves garlic, pressed
Salt and pepper to taste
1/2 cup chopped cilantro leaves

Place all ingredients in large mixing bowl and stir to mix. For salsa, let sit for an hour before serving.

As a warm side dish, simmer all ingredients in a large covered pot with 1 cup chopped fresh greens (spinach, kale, chard) and 1/2 cup uncooked rice. Add tomato juice, veggie broth or water as needed until grains and greens are cooked.

SAUTÉED PEARS AND PEPPERS
A Wing and A Pear

Serves 6

2 tablespoons margarine (lowfat ok)
1 medium red bell pepper, seeded and cut into thin strips
3 medium firm pears, peeled, cored and sliced
1/2 cup shredded Jack cheese (lowfat ok)

Melt 1 tablespoon margarine in large skillet. Add pepper strips and sauté until they begin to soften. Add remaining margarine and pears. Cook, stirring often, until pears are tender.

Transfer to serving dish and sprinkle with cheese.

CHEESY HOMINY CASSEROLE
Homily Hominy

Serves 4-6

2 16-ounce cans white hominy, drained
8 ounces sour cream (lowfat ok)
1 4-ounce can chopped green chilies, drained
2 cups shredded cheddar or Jack cheese (lowfat ok)

Combine all ingredients in 2-quart casserole. Bake at 350°F for 25 minutes. Serve at once.

Gos-Summer Squash

Serves 6

2 tablespoons olive oil
1 large yellow onion, chopped
3 cloves garlic, pressed
3 medium zucchini or yellow squash,
sliced in 1/2-inch thick semi-circles
1 teaspoon dried marjoram
1 16-ounce can chickpeas, drained
1/2 cup salty Greek black olives, pitted and sliced
1 tablespoon ground cumin
Juice of 2 lemons
Salt and freshly ground black pepper, if needed
Pinch cayenne pepper
5 ounces crumbled feta cheese, optional

In large soup pot or Dutch oven over medium heat, sauté onion and garlic until onion is translucent. Add squash and marjoram, cooking until squash is tender.

Add chickpeas, olives, cumin, lemon juice and seasonings. (If using feta, little or no salt will be needed.) Cook until everything is thoroughly heated but squash is not too soft.

Serve over rice or couscous and sprinkle with feta, if desired.

STIR-FRIED ASPARAGUS
Glorious-paragus

Serves 4-6

1 pound fresh asparagus
2 tablespoons oil
1 teaspoon salt
1 teaspoon sugar

Wash asparagus in cold water. Remove tough stem ends. Cut tender parts into 1-inch diamond-shaped pieces by making a diagonal slice, rolling half a turn and slicing again.

Heat oil in very hot skillet or wok. Add asparagus when oil starts smoking. Stir-fry until each piece is coated. Add salt and sugar and stir-fry for 1-2 minutes. Serve hot or cold.

Tidings of Comfort and Bok Joy

Serves 4-6

1 pound broccoli, rinsed in cold water

3 tablespoons vegetable or peanut oil

2 cloves garlic, pressed

1/2 teaspoon salt

1 stalk bok choy, sliced

1/4 teaspoon sugar

3 tablespoons soy sauce or tamari

1/4 cup water

1 teaspoon rice wine or dry sherry, optional

1 tablespoon sesame oil, optional

Cut broccoli into 2-inch flowerets and slice stems 1/4-inch thick. Heat oil in wok or large skillet over high heat for 30 seconds. Stir-fry garlic for 30 seconds. Add stems and salt. Stir-fry 30 seconds.

Add flowerets and bok choy. Stir-fry 1 minute. Add sugar, soy sauce, water and optional wine. Reduce heat to medium low and stir-fry until water is almost gone. Toss with sesame oil, if desired. Serve immediately.

Joyful and Try Eggplant

Makes 4-5 cups

2 tablespoons olive oil

1 medium onion, chopped

1 28-ounce can peeled tomatoes with juice, chopped

1 cup sliced okra, stems removed

1 small green bell pepper, chopped

1 medium eggplant, peeled and chopped

1 medium zucchini, chopped

3 cloves garlic, pressed

1/4 teaspoon dried basil and/or oregano

Salt and pepper to taste

1 bay leaf

In large skillet, sauté onion in oil. Add remaining ingredients. Cook until tender, 20-30 minutes. Remove bay leaf. Serve warm over rice or chill and serve as appetizer with French bread or crackers.

Para-Diced Vegetables

Serves 6

3 medium carrots, thinly sliced

2 medium zucchini, thinly sliced

2 medium tomatoes, peeled and thinly sliced

1/2 medium red onion, thinly sliced

1/2 teaspoon salt

1/4 teaspoon pepper

1/2 cup brown sugar, packed

1 bunch fresh basil leaves, chopped

1/2 cup cracker or bread crumbs

Dabs of margarine (lowfat ok), about 4 teaspoons total

1 cup grated cheddar cheese (lowfat ok)

Layer first 4 ingredients in order in oval or oblong 2-quart casserole. Combine next 5 ingredients in small bowl. Sprinkle over casserole. Dot with margarine and sprinkle with cheese. Bake covered at 350°F for 1/2 hour and uncovered for another 1/2 hour.

Mir-a-Kale Polenta

Serves 4-6

Polenta:

3 cups water

1 cup coarsely ground yellow cornmeal

1/4 teaspoon salt

1/4 cup Parmesan cheese

Kale:

1 tablespoon olive oil

1 large onion, finely chopped

4 cloves garlic, pressed

1/2 pound fresh kale, stems removed and finely chopped

1/4 cup water

Freshly ground pepper to taste

2 tablespoons lemon juice

Salt to taste

2 tablespoons minced fresh parsley or cilantro leaves

2 tablespoons pine nuts, lightly toasted

To make polenta, boil water in heavy saucepan. Gradually add cornmeal, whisking constantly. Add salt and reduce heat. Stir often with a wooden spoon for 15-20 minutes until polenta becomes stiff yet creamy. Stir in Parmesan cheese. Cover and remove from heat.

Heat oil in large skillet over medium heat. Sauté onion until translucent. Stir in garlic and kale. Sauté until leaves begin to wilt. Add water, cover pan and simmer several minutes over low heat until kale is tender. Remove cover and cook away any remaining liquid. Stir in remaining ingredients and set aside.

Stir hot polenta thoroughly and spoon onto plates, making an indentation in center of each serving. Fill with kale mixture.

Blissotto Risotto

Serves 6

8 medium dried shitake mushrooms*
5 cups vegetable bouillon broth
1 tablespoon olive oil
1 medium yellow onion, chopped
4 large cloves garlic, pressed
8 ounces crimini mushrooms, sliced*
1 cup arborio rice*
Salt and freshly ground pepper to taste
2 tablespoons chopped fresh parsley
Grated Parmesan cheese

In medium saucepan, heat shitakes and broth to boiling. Cover, reduce heat and simmer for 10 minutes. Remove from heat and let sit covered for 20 minutes.

Drain mushrooms, reserving broth. Discard shitake stems. Slice caps and set aside. Reheat reserved broth to boiling and simmer.

Heat oil in large saucepan over medium heat. Sauté onion until translucent. Add garlic, crimini and sliced shitake mushrooms. Sauté briefly. Stir in rice. Add 1 cup simmering broth. Cook, stirring, about 5 minutes until rice has absorbed broth. Continue cooking 30 more minutes, adding broth 1 cup at a time as absorbed, stirring often.

Stir in salt, pepper and 1 tablespoon parsley. Garnish each serving with remaining parsley and Parmesan.

*Available in the international aisle or produce sections of larger grocery stores.

Sing in Eggs-ultation

Cantata Frittata

Jacob's Batter

As-Prayer-agus

Join the Triumph of the Pies

Ga-Brie-el Cheese Casserole

Quiche an Angel Good Morning

Ricotta Dump-Wings

Solemn Prayer Camembert

Cantata Frittata

Serves 2-4

1 large thin-skinned potato, peeled and diced
8 ounces mushrooms, thinly sliced
2 teaspoons olive oil
1/2 cup water
2 green onions, thinly sliced
4 large eggs
1 teaspoon fresh chopped dill
1 cup shredded cheddar cheese (lowfat ok)
Salt and pepper

In large skillet with ovenproof handle, briefly sauté potatoes and mushrooms in oil over medium heat. Add 1/4 cup water and cook until potatoes are tender, about 12 minutes.

In mixing bowl, combine onions, eggs, dill, cheese and remaining 1/4 cup water. Pour egg mixture over vegetables. Reduce heat to low and cook until eggs begin to set at edges. Place pan under broiler and broil until eggs feel set when lightly touched. Season with salt and pepper.

Jacob's Batter

Makes 8-10 crêpes

3 eggs
1/2 cup unbleached all-purpose flour
1/4 teaspoon salt
1/2 cup milk (lowfat ok)
1 tablespoon oil
Oil for frying

Filling options:

Ricotta or cottage cheese (lowfat ok),
fresh fruit, jams or preserves, etc.

Beat eggs slightly. Add flour and salt. Stir until batter is smooth. Combine milk and oil. Stir into egg mixture until batter looks like heavy cream. Heat small amount of oil on griddle or skillet over medium-high heat.

For each crêpe, pour about 1/4 cup batter. Turn only once. Fill center with ricotta or cottage cheese and fresh fruit or preserves. Roll up and serve at once.

As-Prayer-agus
Makes 8 crêpes

1 recipe crêpes, prepared and set aside (see page 65)

Sauce:
2 tablespoons margarine (lowfat ok)
2 green onions with tops, chopped
2 cloves garlic, pressed
8 ounces small white or cremini mushrooms, thinly sliced
2 tablespoons unbleached all-purpose flour
1-1/2 cups milk (lowfat ok)
2 tablespoons minced fresh or 1 tablespoon dried dill
1/2 teaspoon dried tarragon
1 tablespoon lemon juice
Salt and freshly ground pepper to taste
48 slender asparagus stalks (about 1 pound),
tough ends trimmed off

Melt margarine in medium saucepan. Add onions and garlic. Sauté for 1 minute. Add mushrooms, cover and cook until juicy. Sprinkle in flour, stirring until it disappears. Slowly pour in milk, stirring. Add dill and tarragon. Simmer until mixture thickens, stirring frequently. Stir in lemon juice, salt and pepper. Remove from heat and cover.

Steam asparagus in vegetable steamer or in microwave until crisp-tender.

To assemble, place 6 stalks in center of each crêpe, letting tips protrude. Spoon small amount of sauce over asparagus. Fold one end of crêpe toward center and overlap the other end. Arrange crêpes, folded side down in greased shallow baking dish. Spoon remaining sauce evenly over crêpes.

Bake at 350°F until just heated through. Serve immediately.

This sauce is heavenly over pasta, too!

Join the Triumph of the Pies

Serves 4-6

2 pounds leeks, ends trimmed

1 large potato, peeled, cooked and mashed

4 eggs

3/4 cup grated Parmesan cheese

Salt to taste

2 tablespoons olive oil

Slice leeks thinly, using white and palest green parts only. In large soup pot, cook leeks in salted water to cover until tender. Drain thoroughly.

Add mashed potato, eggs, cheese and salt, stirring until mixture is uniform. Heat olive oil slightly in 8-inch layer cake pan. Spoon in mixture. Bake at 375°F for 30-40 minutes until top is golden brown. Cut in wedges and serve warm.

Quiche an Angel Good Morning

Makes 2 pies

1 tablespoon margarine
1 10-ounce package frozen chopped spinach,
cooked and drained
1 small onion, chopped
1 small red bell pepper, seeded and diced
2 cloves garlic, pressed
4 eggs
1 13-ounce can evaporated milk (lowfat ok)
Salt and pepper to taste
2 teaspoons dried basil
2 tablespoons toasted pine nuts
1/2 pound Swiss cheese (lowfat ok), grated
3/4 cup grated Parmesan cheese, divided
2 9-inch no-lard pie crusts, unbaked (see page 124)

In skillet, melt margarine. Sauté drained spinach, onion, bell pepper and garlic until onion is translucent. Set aside. In large mixing bowl, beat eggs, milk, salt, black pepper and basil until creamy.

Stir in spinach mixture, pine nuts, Swiss cheese and 1/2 cup Parmesan cheese. Pour equal amounts into pie crusts. Sprinkle remaining Parmesan cheese on top. Bake at 350ºF for 40-45 minutes.

Ricotta Dump-Wings

Serves 4-6

6-8 cups vegetable bouillon broth
1/2 cup grated Parmesan cheese
1/2 cup ricotta cheese (lowfat ok)
1/2 cup unbleached all-purpose flour
1 large egg, lightly beaten
2 tablespoons fresh basil, parsley or cilantro, minced
Green onion tops, thinly sliced

Heat broth until simmering in large pot. In medium bowl, combine the Parmesan cheese, ricotta, flour, egg and herb of choice, stirring just until smooth. Scoop about 1 tablespoon mixture with rounded spoon and with second spoon, smooth top into a dumpling.

Drop into simmering soup and repeat until all dumplings are formed. Simmer until dumplings are cooked through, about 6 minutes. Serve in bowl with broth and top with green onion.

Solemn Prayer Camembert

Serves 24-36

1 loaf crusty French bread, halved lengthwise
3 tablespoons margarine, melted (lowfat ok)
2 teaspoons total any dried herbs
(basil, oregano, rosemary, etc.)
1 16-ounce can whole cranberries, divided
2 large crisp Granny Smith apples, cored and very thinly sliced
8 ounces round Camembert cheese,
quartered and thinly sliced

Score tops of bread halves diagonally to desired serving size for breaking off later. Stir herbs into melted margarine and drizzle or brush 1-1/2 tablespoons over top of each bread half. Spread with thin layer of cranberries, reserving remaining berries. Arrange Camembert slices diagonally, then angle overlapping apple slices over cheese. Top with dollops of remaining cranberries.

Place on baking sheet. Bake at 350°F for 5-10 minutes until cheese begins to melt. Remove from oven and carefully break off pieces.

Ga-Brie-el Cheese Casserole

Serves 4-6

6 ounces brie, frozen and shredded
4 ounces sun-dried tomatoes, softened and sliced
1/2 cup salty Greek black olives, pitted and halved
1/2 cup chopped fresh basil leaves
1/4 cup olive oil
1 clove garlic, pressed
Freshly ground pepper to taste
1 8-ounce package fettucine

In large bowl, combine all ingredients except pasta. Let stand for at least 4 hours. Cook fettucine according to package directions. Drain and place into 2-quart casserole. Toss in brie mixture and serve at once.

For larger gatherings, just double amounts of all ingredients.

Angel Hair & Others

Amen-icotti

Coat of Many Collards

Eternal Ziti Salad

Fettucine Al-Pray-do

Botticelli Vermicelli

Arch-Angel Hair Pasta

Penne from Heaven

Promised Land-guine

Bless-to Pesto

Pasta Prima-Cherub

Cantata Ricotta Shells

Shangri-La-sagna

Far-Fallen Angel

BAKED MANICOTTI

Amen-icotti

Serves 8

1 8-ounce package manicotti shells
1 32-ounce jar extra thick spaghetti sauce
2 cups shredded mozzarella cheese (lowfat ok)
1 16-ounce carton ricotta cheese (lowfat ok)
12 2-inch saltine crackers, crushed
2 eggs, beaten
1/4 cup chives, chopped
1/2 teaspoon dried basil
1/2 teaspoon dried marjoram
1/4 teaspoon garlic salt

Cook shells and drain. Pour half of spaghetti sauce into lightly greased 9x13-inch baking dish. In large bowl, combine 1-1/2 cups mozzarella and remaining ingredients. Mix well.

Stuff shells with cheese mixture and arrange in prepared dish over sauce. Pour remaining sauce over manicotti, and bake at 350°F for 25 minutes. Sprinkle with remaining 1/2 cup mozzarella. Bake additional 5 minutes.

Coat of Many Collards

Serves 6

2 tablespoons olive oil
1 medium yellow onion, chopped
1 clove garlic, pressed
4 cups collard greens, washed, dried and well chopped
1 tablespoon lemon juice
Salt to taste
1 8-ounce package small pasta shells
1 cup ricotta cheese (lowfat ok)
Grated Parmesan cheese to taste
Freshly ground black pepper to taste
Dash nutmeg, optional

Heat oil in Dutch oven over medium heat. Add onion and sauté until translucent. Add garlic, collards, lemon juice and salt. Stir-fry until greens wilt. Cover and cook 8-10 minutes over low heat.

Cook pasta according to package directions. Drain and set aside. Add ricotta cheese to greens, mixing well. Stir in pasta until thoroughly mixed. Add Parmesan cheese, pepper and nutmeg, if desired. Mix well and serve at once.

Eternal Ziti Salad

Makes 4 servings

Dressing:

1/3 cup balsamic or red wine vinegar
1-1/2 tablespoons Dijon mustard
2 teaspoons dry tarragon, basil or dill
3 tablespoons olive oil
Salt to taste

Salad:

1 8-ounce package ziti (mostaccioli)
1 large head red leaf lettuce, rinsed and dried
8 medium-sized Roma (plum) tomatoes, thinly-sliced
2/3 cup crumbled feta cheese
1/2 cup salty Greek black olives
Freshly ground pepper to taste

In small bowl, combine dressing ingredients and mix well. Set aside. Cook pasta according to package directions. Drain, rinse with cold water and drain again. Place in large mixing bowl. Toss 1/3 cup dressing into pasta.

Tear lettuce into bite-sized pieces and arrange on four dinner plates. Mound pasta on lettuce and top with tomatoes. Sprinkle with cheese and olives. Drizzle remaining dressing over salads. Season with pepper.

Fettucine Al-Pray-do

Serves 6

1 8-ounce package fettucine

1/3 cup milk (lowfat ok)

1 cup ricotta cheese (lowfat ok)

1 egg yolk

1/4 teaspoon freshly ground black pepper

2 tablespoons margarine, melted (lowfat ok)

1/2 cup grated Parmesan cheese, divided

Dash nutmeg, optional

Cook fettucine according to package directions. Drain and set aside. In food processor or blender, blend milk, ricotta cheese, egg and pepper. In saucepan, melt margarine over low heat. Add cheese mixture and bring to a simmer, stirring occasionally.

Stir in all but 6 teaspoons Parmesan cheese. Pour mixture over fettucine and toss. Sprinkle each serving with remaining Parmesan cheese and dash nutmeg, if desired.

Botticelli Vermicelli

Serves 4-6

2 tablespoons sesame oil

3 tablespoons tahini (sesame paste)

2 tablespoons peanut butter

2 tablespoons tamari or soy sauce

2 cloves garlic, pressed

1/4 teaspoon grated fresh ginger root

1/8 teaspoon cayenne pepper or to taste

3 teaspoons brown sugar

2 teaspoons rice vinegar

3 tablespoons green onion tops, thinly sliced

1 8-ounce package vermicelli cooked, drained and cooled

In food processor or blender, blend all ingredients except 1 tablespoon green onions and vermicelli. Blend until creamy. Thin with small amount of water if too thick. Toss into vermicelli and garnish with remaining green onions.

Arch-Angel Hair Pasta

Serves 6

2 tablespoons margarine (lowfat ok)
1/4 cup chopped green onions
2 cloves garlic, pressed
1/2 cup softened sun-dried tomatoes, chopped
1 14-1/2-ounce can peeled tomatoes, chopped (juice reserved)
1 bunch fresh basil leaves, chopped or 1 tablespoon dried
Salt and freshly ground pepper to taste
8 ounces fresh or dry angel hair pasta
Grated Parmesan cheese

Melt margarine in large skillet over low heat. Sauté green onions, garlic and sun-dried tomatoes for 1 minute. Add canned tomatoes, basil, salt and pepper. Simmer about 5 minutes. Add small amount of reserved tomato juice to desired consistency. Remove from heat.

Prepare pasta according to package directions and drain. Toss sauce with hot pasta and serve immediately. Sprinkle each serving with Parmesan cheese and pepper.

For an interesting touch, add 1 cup chopped, marinated artichoke hearts with the canned tomatoes.

Penne from Heaven

Serves 6

3 tablespoons margarine

1/2 cup pine nuts

1/2 cup seasoned bread crumbs

1 medium clove garlic, pressed

1 tablespoon chopped parsley

1 8-ounce package penne pasta

Melt margarine in small pan over low heat. Add pine nuts, bread crumbs and garlic. Stir frequently until nuts and crumbs are golden brown. Stir in parsley and cook for 30 seconds. Remove from heat.

Cook pasta according to package directions. Drain and place in serving bowl. Toss nut mixture gently into penne.

Promised Land-guine

Serves 6

3 tablespoons margarine (lowfat ok)
3 cups sliced mushrooms
2 cups sour cream (lowfat ok)
1 tablespoon dry onion bouillon
1 teaspoon garlic powder
1 tablespoon tamari or soy sauce, optional
1 8-ounce package linguine, cooked and drained
Dash paprika

Heat margarine in large skillet. Sauté mushrooms. Place sour cream in mixing bowl. Stir in bouillon, garlic powder and tamari, if desired Mix thoroughly.

When mushrooms are soft, pour sour cream mixture into skillet. Stir to mix. Let mixture heat slightly, do not overheat. Toss over noodles and sprinkle with paprika.

BASIL PESTO

Bless-to Pesto

Makes about 3 cups

2 cups fresh basil leaves
4 medium cloves garlic, chopped
1 cup walnuts or pine nuts
1/4 cup olive oil
1 cup Parmesan cheese, grated
Salt and freshly ground black pepper, to taste

Process the basil, garlic and walnuts or pine nuts in food processor or blender. With machine running, add oil in steady stream. Add cheese, pinch of salt and pepper to taste. If too thick, add water by teaspoons and blend until desired consistency is reached.

Place in bowl and cover until ready to use. Store in refrigerator. Serve over hot, fresh pasta.

On the other side: For a reduced fat pesto, reduce olive oil to one teaspoon and thin with water. For a creamy pesto, blend in 4 ounces lowfat cream cheese.

Pasta Prima-Cherub

Serves 4-6

1 16-ounce bag frozen Italian style vegetables
2 tablespoons cornstarch
1-1/2 cups vegetable bouillon broth
1 16-ounce package spaghetti, cooked and drained
1 cup grated Parmesan cheese

Steam or microwave vegetables until just tender.
Cover and set aside. In saucepan over medium heat, combine
cornstarch with 1/4 cup broth. Stir until cornstarch dissolves.
Add remaining broth and bring to boil. Reduce heat, stirring
constantly until thickened.

In large serving bowl, toss
vegetables, sauce, pasta
and Parmesan cheese.
Mix thoroughly and serve
promptly.

Cantata Ricotta Shells

Serves 6

3 cups ricotta cheese (lowfat ok)

1 cup grated Parmesan cheese, divided

1 10-1/2 ounce package frozen chopped spinach,

thawed and drained

1 egg

1/4 teaspoon salt

1/2 teaspoon black pepper

1 teaspoon garlic powder

Dash nutmeg

1 12-ounce package jumbo shells, cooked and drained

3 cups spaghetti sauce

Combine first 8 ingredients in mixing bowl. Stuff shells with mixture. Cover bottom of baking dish with 1 cup spaghetti sauce. Arrange stuffed shells in dish and pour remaining spaghetti sauce over all. Cover and bake 25 minutes at 350°F. Uncover and sprinkle with remaining Parmesan cheese. Bake 5 more minutes.

MEATLESS LASAGNA

Shangri-La-sagna

Serves 12

2 cups ricotta cheese (lowfat ok)
1 cup cottage cheese (lowfat ok)
1 tablespoon dried basil
1 tablespoon dried parsley
1 teaspoon garlic powder
4 cups bottled spaghetti sauce
1 cup grated mozzarella cheese (lowfat ok)
3/4 pound lasagna noodles, uncooked
1/2 cup grated Parmesan cheese

Preheat oven to 350°F. In large bowl, combine first 5 ingredients. Pour 1 cup spaghetti sauce in bottom of greased 9x13-inch baking dish. Arrange 1 layer of noodles over sauce. Top with 1/2 of the ricotta mixture and sprinkle with 1/2 cup mozzarella cheese.

Continue layering 1 cup spaghetti sauce, 1 layer noodles, remaining ricotta mixture and mozzarella cheese. Add another cup of sauce, layer of noodles and remaining sauce. Sprinkle with Parmesan cheese. Cover tightly with lid or aluminum foil. Bake for one hour.

FARFALLE WITH WILD MUSHROOMS
Far-Fallen Angel
Serves 6

8 ounces farfalle (bow tie) pasta
2 cloves garlic, pressed
1 pound total fresh wild mushrooms, thinly sliced
(shitake, portabella, cremini, oyster, etc.)*
2 tablespoons margarine (lowfat ok)
1-2 tablespoons soy sauce or tamari
Freshly ground black pepper to taste
Grated Parmesan cheese

Prepare pasta according to package directions. Drain and set aside in large covered casserole.

In large skillet, melt margarine over medium heat. Sauté garlic for 1 minute. Add mushrooms. Stir well to coat and sauté until mushrooms become slightly juicy. Stir in soy sauce or tamari to taste. Season with black pepper.

Pour mushroom mixture over pasta and toss thoroughly. Serve immediately and top each serving with grated Parmesan.

*Available in the international aisle or produce sections of larger grocery stores.

MAIN DISHES
Main-gels

Celestial Chili

O Ta-ma-le Faithful

Miracle Mexi-Corn

Heavenly Helper

Angel-adas

Nirvana Moussaka

Wish-Kebobs

Angel Baby

Ha-Lo Mein

In Excelsius Mayo

Gabriel-a Portabella

Egg-Chant Parmesan

Stuffed Di-Vine Leaves

Shepherd's Pie

Raphael Falafel

A Toast of Angels

Celestial Chili

Serves 8-10

2 tablespoons olive oil

1 large onion, chopped

5 medium garlic cloves, pressed

3 tablespoons cumin

2 cups chopped zucchini

1 28-ounce can undrained tomatoes, coarsely chopped

1 medium red bell pepper, seeded and chopped

Jalapeño pepper to taste, seeded and minced

2 15-ounce cans black beans, drained

1/2 cup chopped cilantro leaves

3 tablespoons fresh lime juice

Salt and black pepper to taste

In large pot, heat oil over low heat. Sauté onion, garlic and cumin until onion is translucent. Add zucchini, tomatoes, bell and jalapeño peppers, beans and cilantro. Cover and let simmer for 45 minutes, stirring occasionally. Just before serving, stir in lime juice, salt and black pepper.

TAMALE CORNBREAD PIE

O Ta-ma-le Faithful

Serves 16

1 recipe cornbread batter without cheese (see page 139)
1 16-ounce can kidney beans with liquid
1/2 cup chopped onion
1/2 cup chopped green bell pepper
1 4-ounce can chopped chilies
1 medium tomato, diced
1/4 cup chopped black olives
1 cup corn
1 clove garlic, pressed
1 teaspoon cumin
2 teaspoons chili powder
Salt to taste
1 cup grated sharp cheese (lowfat ok)
Salsa

Prepare cornbread batter and set aside. In medium saucepan, simmer beans with liquid, vegetables and spices for 10 minutes. Stir in half the cheese. Spread half the cornbread batter into oiled 9x13-inch baking pan.

Top with hot bean mixture then rest of batter. Bake at 425°F for 15 minutes. Sprinkle on remaining cheese and bake 10 more minutes. Serve with salsa.

Miracle Mexi-Corn

Serves 6-8

3 cups cooked rice (quick-cooking type ok)
2 cups sour cream (lowfat ok)
5 green onions, chopped
Salt and pepper to taste
1 14-1/2-ounce can corn, drained
1 4-ounce can mild green chilies, drained
1 cup shredded Jack cheese (lowfat ok)
1/4 cup shredded cheddar cheese (lowfat ok)
3 tablespoons chopped fresh cilantro

Preheat oven to 350°F. In large bowl, mix rice and sour cream. Stir in green onions, salt and pepper. Spread 1/2 rice mixture in bottom of greased 2-quart casserole. Top with half the corn, half the chilies and half the Jack cheese.

Repeat with remaining rice, corn, chilies and Jack cheese. Top with cheddar cheese. Bake covered for 20 minutes, uncovered for 10 more minutes. Sprinkle with cilantro and serve.

Heavenly Helper

Makes about 2 cups

2 tablespoons oil
1 medium yellow onion, diced
3 cloves garlic, minced
1/4 cup chopped green pepper
1 cup bulghur (cracked) wheat
1 cup bottled salsa
1-2 cups tomato juice
3 tablespoons taco seasoning mix

In large skillet heat oil over medium heat. Sauté onion, garlic and green pepper until tender. Add bulghur. Sauté 1 minute, stirring well.

Stir in salsa, 1 cup tomato juice and taco seasoning. Cover and reduce heat. Let simmer, stirring occasionally. Cook for 10-15 minutes until mixture is slightly chewy, adding more tomato juice if necessary.

Angel-adas

Makes 10-12 enchiladas

1 recipe "Heavenly Helper", warm (see page 91)
10-12 medium-sized soft flour tortillas
1 cup bottled salsa
1-1/2 cups grated Jack or cheddar cheese (lowfat ok)
Chopped cilantro leaves for garnish

Fill tortillas one at a time with 2-3 tablespoons Mexican filling and sprinkle with 2 tablespoons cheese. Roll up and place seam side down into a large shallow baking dish. Top with salsa and cheese. Bake at 350°F for 20 minutes. Garnish with cilantro.

Nirvana Moussaka

Serves 6-8

1 large eggplant, peeled
2 cups cooked rice (quick-cooking type ok)
3 cups bottled spaghetti sauce
1/2 cup chopped parsley or cilantro
1/4 teaspoon cinnamon
Salt and pepper to taste
1 15-ounce carton ricotta cheese (lowfat ok)
1 12-ounce can evaporated milk (lowfat ok)
1 cup grated Parmesan cheese, divided
1/8 teaspoon nutmeg or more to taste
Seasoned bread crumbs

Cut eggplant into thin slices. In large bowl, stir together rice, spaghetti sauce, parsley or cilantro, cinnamon, salt and pepper. In blender or food processor, blend ricotta cheese, evaporated milk, 1/2 cup Parmesan cheese and nutmeg.

Preheat oven to 375°F. Grease a 3-quart baking dish and sprinkle bottom lightly with bread crumbs. Alternate layers of eggplant and rice mixture, sprinkling each layer lightly with remaining Parmesan cheese and bread crumbs. Pour ricotta mixture over top of casserole and bake 45-55 minutes or until top is golden.

Wish-Kebobs

Serves 4

Marinade:

3 cloves garlic, pressed

1 teaspoon onion powder

1/4 teaspoon ground oregano

1 tablespoon soy sauce or tamari

2 tablespoons rice vinegar or lemon juice

8 ounces firm tofu

2 cups cubed vegetables/fruits (onion, zucchini, bell pepper, eggplant, pineapple, whole cherry tomatoes)

Olive oil

Mix marinade ingredients in bowl. On large plate, wrap tofu with paper towels. Top with large plate. Let drain for 10 minutes. Cut tofu into 2-inch cubes. Place in marinade for 30 minutes, turning frequently.

Preheat broiler or grill. Alternate tofu, vegetables and/or fruit on skewers. Brush all lightly with olive oil. Broil or grill until lightly browned. Serve hot.

Angel Baby

Serves 6

1 cup whole dried shitake mushrooms*
2 tablespoons vegetable or peanut oil
2 thin slices fresh ginger root, peeled
1/2 teaspoon salt
1 teaspoon soy sauce
1 15-ounce can baby corn, drained
2 cups snow peas, strings removed
1 teaspoon cornstarch
1 teaspoon sugar

Soak mushrooms in water to cover for 30 minutes until soft. Reserve liquid. Dry mushrooms and cut off tough stems.

Heat wok or large skillet and add oil. When hot, swirl ginger around bottom, then discard ginger. Add mushrooms and stir-fry for about 2 minutes. Add 1 tablespoon mushroom liquid, salt and soy sauce. Stir for 1 minute.

Add baby corn and pea pods. Stir-fry for 2 minutes, then add 3 more tablespoons mushroom liquid. In small bowl, blend 3 tablespoons mushroom liquid, cornstarch and sugar. Add to vegetable mixture and stir in well. Let thicken slightly. Serve at once.

*Available in the international aisle or produce sections of larger grocery stores.

VEGETABLE LO MEIN
Ha-Lo Mein

Serves 6

1/2 pound spaghetti, broken in half
1 recipe "Angel Baby" (see page 95)
Soy sauce and/or sesame oil, optional

Cook noodles al dente and drain. Combine noodles and vegetables in serving bowl and toss well. Season with soy sauce and/or sesame oil, if desired.

GARLIC MAYONNAISE
In Excelsius Mayo

Makes 1/4 cup

4 tablespoons mayonnaise (lowfat ok)
1 clove garlic, pressed
1/4 teaspoon dried parsley or basil

Mix ingredients in small bowl. Keep chilled before serving.

Gabriel-a Portabella

Serves 4

4 large portabella mushroom caps, stems removed
Olive oil or margarine
4 thin slices mozzarella or Jack cheese (lowfat ok)
4 large roasted red pepper or marinated pimiento slices
4 hamburger or other buns
Garlic mayonnaise (see page 96)
Salt and freshly ground black pepper to taste

If grilling, lightly brush both sides of mushrooms with olive oil. Place on medium-hot grill. Turn and brush often with oil until mushrooms are streaked with brown and getting juicy. If cooking indoors, sauté mushrooms in large skillets with 1 tablespoon margarine per skillet. Turn and cook until juicy.

Spread buns lightly with garlic mayonnaise. Place portabella on bottom bun. Top with cheese and roasted pepper slice. Season with salt and pepper if needed.

Egg-Chant Parmesan

Serves 8-12

1 large eggplant, peeled and thinly sliced
Salt
1 48-ounce jar spaghetti sauce (about 4 cups)
1 cup seasoned finely-ground bread crumbs
2 teaspoons dried basil
2 cups shredded mozzarella cheese (lowfat ok)
1-1/2 cups grated Parmesan cheese

On paper towels, arrange eggplant in single layer. Lightly salt one side. Top with paper towels then weight with heavy plates or cutting board. Let sit for at least 30 minutes to remove bitter liquid. Pat dry.

In 9x13-inch baking pan, pour 1 cup sauce. Arrange single layer of eggplant. Sprinkle lightly with 1/3 cup bread crumbs, 1 cup sauce, 1 teaspoon basil, 1 cup mozzarella and 1/2 cup Parmesan. Repeat layers, omitting mozzarella for top layer.

Cover and bake at 350°F for 30 minutes. Uncover and bake for 15-25 minutes more until eggplant is tender.

Stuffed Di-Vine Leaves

Serves 6

2 tablespoons olive oil

1/2 cup minced onion

2 cloves garlic, pressed

1 cup rice

Juice of 1 lemon

2 cups vegetable bouillon broth

2 teaspoons dried or 2 tablespoons fresh parsley, minced

1 tablespoon soy sauce or tamari, optional

1/2 teaspoon freshly ground black pepper

1 8-ounce jar grape (vine) leaves (use about 15-20 leaves)

In large skillet over low heat, sauté onion and garlic in 1 tablespoon oil until onion is translucent. Add rice and sauté briefly. Stir in lemon juice and broth. Cover and simmer until rice is cooked according to package directions.

Remove from heat and stir in remaining olive oil, parsley, optional soy sauce and black pepper. Preheat oven to 350°F. Wash brine off leaves.

To fill, place leaf flat with stem facing you. Place 1-2 table-spoons filling in center and fold stem over it. Fold the two sides into the center, and working from the end closest to you, roll leaf until it is completely wrapped around the filling.

Place seam side down in lightly greased 9x13-inch baking pan. Bake for 15-20 minutes. Serve immediately. Top with lemon sesame dressing (page 34) or plain lowfat yogurt.

Shepherd's Pie

Serves 6

1 medium yellow onion
1 tablespoon olive oil
1 head cauliflower, cut into florets
1 large potato, peeled and diced
1 16-ounce can peeled tomatoes with juice, chopped
1 carrot diced
Salt to taste
1 tablespoon curry mix (see page 48)
1 4-ounce can chopped green chilies

Topping:

4 cups mashed potatoes
1/4 teaspoon turmeric
1/4 teaspoon cumin

In soup pot or Dutch oven, sauté onion and garlic in oil until golden. Add cauliflower and sauté 5 more minutes. Stir in diced potato, tomatoes, carrot, salt, spice mix and chilies until well mixed. Bring to a boil, then cover and simmer over low heat about 15 minutes. Transfer vegetable mixture to a 3-quart casserole.

Stir topping spices into mashed potatoes. Spread mashed potatoes over top of casserole, sealing at edges. Bake at 350°F about 15 minutes.

FALAFEL PATTIES

Raphael Falafel

Serves 6

3 slices firm whole wheat bread, crustless
2 tablespoons fresh lemon juice
2 tablespoons unbleached all-purpose flour
2 tablespoons tahini (sesame paste) or olive oil
3 garlic cloves, pressed
1 egg
2 tablespoons chopped parsley
1/4 teaspoon salt
1/4 teaspoon black pepper
1/2 teaspoon ground cumin
1/4 teaspoon basil
Cayenne pepper to taste
1 15-ounce can chickpeas, drained
Oil or margarine for frying
Lowfat plain yogurt for topping

In blender or food processor, blend all ingredients except chickpeas until smooth. Add chickpeas and blend only to a rough consistency — not too smooth.

Heat 1-2 tablespoons of oil or margarine in skillet or griddle. Pour 1/3 cup mixture on skillet for each pattie. Brown each side. Serve with yogurt.

A Toast of Angels

Serves 4

3 eggs
1 cup milk (lowfat ok)
8 diagonally-cut slices large French bread
(about 1/3 inch thick)
1 cup shredded Jack cheese (lowfat ok)
1 4-ounce can chopped green chilies
1/4 cup minced cilantro
2 cups salsa (see page 15)

Beat eggs and milk in large bowl until blended. Dip 4 slices of bread into egg mixture. Arrange on a greased baking sheet.

Top prepared bread evenly with cheese, chilies and cilantro. Dip remaining bread slices into egg mixture, coating both sides well. Cover each sandwich with a second slice.

Bake at 400°F until sandwiches begin to brown, 10-12 minutes. Turn carefully with spatula. Continue to bake until sandwiches are evenly browned. Transfer to plate and serve with salsa.

O Yum All Ye Platefuls

Judgment Date Bars

Meringue Clouds

Angelic Apricot Bars

Seventh Heaven Layer Cookies

Atone-Mint Brownies

Chow Mein-gels

Heavenly Mess-Ginger

Vir-Chews

Judgment Date Bars

Makes 16 squares

1 cup pitted dates
2 cups shelled pecans or walnuts
1 cup raisins
8 ounces dried figs

In food processor, combine all ingredients. Process until finely chopped. Press into a greased 8x8-inch baking pan and cut into squares.

Meringue Clouds

Makes 5 dozen

4 egg whites
Pinch salt
1 teaspoon vanilla
1 cup sugar
3/4 cup chopped nuts or mini chocolate chips

Preheat oven to 250°F. In mixing bowl, beat egg whites and salt until stiff peaks form. Add vanilla and beat again. Add sugar in small quantities, mixing thoroughly.

Fold in nuts or chocolate chips. Drop batter from a teaspoon onto foil-covered cookie sheet. Bake for 45 minutes in center of oven. Let cool in dry place. Store in airtight container.

Angelic Apricot Bars

Makes 16-24 bars

1/3 cup uncooked oats

1/3 cup unbleached all-purpose flour

1/3 cup brown sugar

1 teaspoon ground cinnamon

1/2 teaspoon baking powder

1/4 teaspoon salt

1/3 cup honey

2 eggs

2 cups chopped diced apricots (about 1 pound)

2 tablespoons chopped walnuts

Powdered sugar for dusting top

Preheat oven to 350°F. In a bowl, combine first 6 ingredients. In large mixing bowl or food processor, mix honey and eggs until frothy. Add dry mixture to wet. Add apricots and walnuts and mix until a thick batter is formed.

Spread into a greased 8x8-inch baking pan. Bake 30-35 minutes or until a toothpick inserted in center comes out clean. Cool on a wire rack. Dust top with powdered sugar and cut into bars.

Seventh Heaven Cookies

Makes about 3 dozen

1/4 cup margarine
1-1/2 cups graham cracker crumbs
1 cup semi-sweet chocolate chips
1 cup shredded coconut
1 cup butterscotch chips
1 cup pecans, chopped
1 14-ounce can sweetened condensed milk

Preheat oven to 350°F. Melt margarine in 9x13-inch baking pan. Sprinkle crumbs evenly over margarine. Layer chocolate chips, coconut, butterscotch chips and pecans.

Pour condensed milk evenly over top of layers. Bake for 30-35 minutes. While still warm, cut into squares. Cool in pan on wire rack.

Chow Mein-gels

Makes about 3 dozen

1 12-ounce package butterscotch or chocolate chips
1 5-ounce can chow mein noodles
1/3 cup pecans or walnuts, finely chopped

Melt chips in large casserole in microwave or in large bowl over boiling water. Gently stir in noodles and nuts.

Drop by tablespoons onto wax paper and refrigerate.

These two recipes are a bit devilish, so make them small.

Heavenly Mess-Ginger

Makes 3-4 dozen

1/4 cup margarine, melted

1/4 cup sugar

1-3/4 cups packed brown sugar

2 eggs

1 teaspoon vanilla

1/4 cup molasses

2 cups unbleached all-purpose flour

2 teaspoons baking powder

3/4 teaspoon ginger

1 teaspoon cinnamon

1/4 teaspoon cloves

1 cup currants or raisins

In large bowl, stir together margarine, sugar and brown sugar. Add eggs and beat. Stir in vanilla and molasses.

In separate bowl, mix flour, baking powder and spices. Add to molasses mixture and mix thoroughly. Stir in currants or raisins. Spread batter in greased 9x13-inch baking pan.

Bake for 20-25 minutes at 350°F. Remove from oven and cool in pan on wire rack. Cut into bars.

Vir-Chews

Makes 4-5 dozen

1 package deluxe moist lemon cake mix
1 8-ounce carton lowfat lemon yogurt
1 egg, beaten slightly
3/4 cup flaked coconut
1/2 teaspoon grated lemon rind

Preheat oven to 350°F. In large bowl, combine dry cake mix, yogurt and egg. Mix until well blended. Stir in coconut and lemon rind.

On lightly greased baking sheets, drop about 1/2 tablespoon cookie dough. Bake about 12-14 minutes until golden. Let cool for one minute. Remove and cool on wire racks.

Atone~Mint Brownies

Makes 3 to 4 dozen

1 package deluxe fudge cake mix
1 8-ounce carton lowfat vanilla yogurt
1 egg, beaten slightly
1/2 cup chopped walnuts
1/2 cup chocolate mint or semi-sweet chocolate chips

Preheat oven to 350°F. In large bowl, combine dry cake mix, yogurt and egg. Mix until well blended. Stir in nuts.

Pour batter into greased 9x13-inch baking pan. Sprinkle with chocolate chips. Bake for 20-25 minutes or until set. Cool in pan on wire rack. Cut into small squares.

For Heaven's Cake

Adam's Apple

Seraphim Cinnamon Treat

Chariot Carrot Cake

Angel Wing Icing

Afterlife Appleloaf

Hark the Cherry Angel Ring

In Cinnamon and Error Pining

Amazing Glaze

Shepherds Quake Cheesecake

Guardian Angel Food Cake

APPLESAUCE SPICE CAKE

Adam's Apple

Serves 24-36

2 cups unbleached all-purpose flour
1-1/2 cups brown sugar, packed
1 teaspoon baking powder
1-1/4 teaspoons baking soda
3/4 teaspoon ground cloves
1/2 teaspoon nutmeg
2 teaspoons cinnamon
2 cups applesauce
2 ripe bananas, peeled
1 cup raisins
1/2 cup chopped walnuts

Preheat oven to 350°F. In large bowl, mix first 7 ingredients. In separate bowl, beat applesauce and bananas until creamy. Stir in raisins and nuts. Mix wet and dry mixtures thoroughly.

Pour batter into a greased 9x13-inch baking pan. Bake for 40-45 minutes until a toothpick or fork inserted in center comes out clean. Let cool.

If desired, top with orange glaze (see page 119).

Seraphim Cinnamon Treat

Serves 4-6

1 cup sugar
1-1/4 cups unbleached all-purpose flour
2 teaspoons baking powder
3 tablespoons margarine, divided
3/4 cup milk (lowfat ok)
1/3 cup brown sugar
1/2 teaspoon cinnamon

Preheat oven to 350°F. In mixing bowl, stir together first 3 ingredients. Cut in 1 tablespoon margarine with fork or pastry blender. Add milk. Mix all together. Pour into greased pie pan. Sprinkle brown sugar and cinnamon on top. Dot with remaining margarine. Bake 30 minutes.

Chariot Carrot Cake

Makes 1 cake or 2 loaves

2-1/2 cups unbleached all-purpose flour

1-1/2 teaspoons baking soda

2 teaspoons baking powder

1/2 teaspoon nutmeg

2 teaspoons cinnamon

1/2 teaspoon ground ginger

1 teaspoon salt

1 cup honey

1/2 cup brown sugar, packed

1 cup buttermilk

2 eggs

3/4 cup applesauce

1 teaspoon vanilla

2 cups grated carrots

1/2 cup raisins

1 cup chopped nuts

Preheat oven to 325°F. Combine first 7 ingredients in large bowl. Using food processor or mixer, blend honey, brown sugar, buttermilk, eggs, applesauce and vanilla. Stir in remaining ingredients.

Mix wet and dry ingredients thoroughly. Pour batter into a greased and floured 9x13-inch pan or 2 9x5-inch loaf pans. Bake for 35-40 minutes until a toothpick or fork inserted in center comes out clean. Cool in pan for 15 minutes, then remove and cool thoroughly on wire rack.

Frost with cream cheese icing, if desired.

CREAM CHEESE ICING

Angel Wing Icing

Frosts 1 9x13-inch cake

1/4 cup margarine, softened

1 8-ounce package cream cheese, softened

1 16-ounce package powdered sugar

1 teaspoon vanilla

In large mixing bowl, beat margarine and cream cheese until fluffy. Add powdered sugar and vanilla. Mix well.

Afterlife Appleloaf

Serves 6

2 cups diced, peeled Granny Smith apples

1 cup sugar

1/4 cup oil

1 egg, beaten

1 teaspoon vanilla

1 cup unbleached all-purpose flour

1 teaspoon baking soda

1 teaspoon cinnamon

1/4 teaspoon salt

1/2 cup chopped nuts, optional

Toss apples and sugar together in medium bowl. Stir in oil, egg and vanilla. In separate bowl, combine flour, baking soda, cinnamon and salt. Mix wet and dry mixtures. Stir in nuts, if desired.

Preheat oven to 350°F. Pour batter into a 9x5-inch loaf pan. Bake for 25-30 minutes.

Hark the Cherry Angel Ring

Serves 6-8

1 17-ounce can pitted bing cherries,
drained with juice reserved
1 3-ounce package Kosher cherry gelatin*
1 12-ounce carton frozen lowfat whipped topping, thawed
1 prepared angel food cake, torn in small pieces
Candied or other cherry halves for decorating, optional

In 2-cup glass measure, place cherry juice and add water to make 1 cup. Heat to boiling and stir in gelatin until dissolved. Transfer to large bowl. Stir in cherries and chill until partially set. Fold in 2 cups whipped topping.

Put one layer of torn cake in bottom of angel food pan. Cover with layer of cherry mixture, then repeat layers. With rubber spatula, push cake so sauce covers all cake pieces. Refrigerate 6 hours or more.

Unmold cake and frost with remaining whipped topping. Arrange cherries on top, if desired.

*Vegetarian note: Kosher gelatin is not made from animal products like regular gelatin. It is found in the international section of many grocery and health food stores.

In Cinnamon and Error Pining

Serves 24-36

1 20-ounce can unsweetened crushed pineapple, undrained

2 eggs, slightly beaten

1 tablespoon lemon juice

1/2 teaspoon grated lemon rind

1/4 teaspoon salt

2 cups unbleached all-purpose flour

1 cup sugar

1 teaspoon cinnamon

2 teaspoons baking soda

1 cup fresh blueberries, stems removed

Preheat oven to 350°F. In large bowl, stir together pineapple, eggs, lemon juice and rind. In separate bowl, combine salt, flour, sugar, cinnamon and baking soda.

Stir dry mixture into wet until mixed. Fold in blueberries. Pour into a 9x13-inch greased baking pan.

Bake for 20-30 minutes. Cool in pan on wire rack. Top with orange glaze (see page 119).

Amazing Glaze

1/4 cup orange juice
1 cup powdered sugar

Mix both ingredients until smooth. Let sit for 5 minutes. Drizzle over cake.

Shepherds Quake Cheesecake

Serves 8-12

Crust:

2/3 cup unbleached all-purpose flour

1/3 cup sugar

1/4 cup margarine, softened

1/2 teaspoon vanilla

Filling:

3 cups fresh berries

or

1 12-ounce package frozen berries, unthawed

2 cups lowfat vanilla yogurt

1 8-ounce package cream cheese (lowfat ok)

Juice and some pulp of 1/2 lemon

2 tablespoons unbleached all-purpose flour

1 egg, slightly beaten

1/3 cup sugar

1 teaspoon vanilla

Preheat oven to 350°F. Combine crust ingredients in large bowl. Mix well and press into 9-inch springform pan. Sprinkle evenly with berries.

Combine remaining ingredients in large bowl. Mix until smooth. Pour over berries. Bake 50-60 minutes until golden and toothpick or fork inserted in center comes out clean.

Let cool at least 30 minutes on wire rack before removing ring. Refrigerate until served.

Guardian Angel Food Cake

Makes 2 loaf cakes

1 angel food cake mix
1/2 cup diced fresh strawberries
1 quart carton lowfat frozen strawberry yogurt, softened
1 12-ounce carton frozen lowfat whipped topping,
thawed before serving
Sliced strawberries for decorating

Prepare angel food batter. Fold in diced strawberries. Pour into 2 9x5-inch loaf pans. Bake and cool according to package directions.

Remove cakes from pan. Cut each lengthwise into 3 even pieces. Spread 2 cups softened yogurt over layer of cake and top with cake layer. Repeat with one more layer yogurt and cake. For second cake, repeat steps.

Before serving, frost with whipped topping and arrange remaining strawberries on top. Freeze any remaining servings (if there are any).

On the other side: Try different frozen yogurt flavors.

Divine Desserts

Heavenly Trust Crust

Amazing Graham

Blueberry Bliss

Preach Cobbler

Sublime Key Lime Pie

Micro-Wing Custard

Cherub Cherry Treat

Lemons We Have Curd on High

Rhub-Harp Crisp

Heaven Flan Wait

Michael-an-Gelato

Prayerful Pear-ful

Heavenly Hash

Divine Divinity

Heavenly Trust Crust

Makes 2 9-inch pie crusts

2 cups unbleached all-purpose flour
1 teaspoon salt
1/2 cup canola oil
1/4 cup cold water
2 9-inch pie plates

Mix flour and salt in bowl. Combine oil and water and mix into flour with fork. Form into 2 balls with hands. Cover with a cloth and let sit for 5 minutes. Roll out between sheets of waxed paper. Place rolled dough into pie plates.

To prebake pie crusts, prick with fork and bake at 375°F for 10-12 minutes.

Amazing Graham

Makes 1 9-inch pie crust

1 cup finely-ground graham cracker crumbs
2 tablespoons sugar
1/4 cup margarine, melted

Combine crumbs and sugar. Add melted margarine and mix well. With back of spoon, press firmly on bottom and sides of 9-inch pie pan. Bake at 300°F for 5-8 minutes. Allow to cool before filling.

Blueberry Bliss

Serves 6

3/4 cup unbleached all-purpose flour
3/4 cup brown sugar
6 tablespoons margarine, softened
1 21-ounce can blueberry pie filling

Preheat oven to 375°F. Mix together flour, brown sugar and margarine until mixture resembles coarse meal. Set aside.

Place pie filling in greased 2-quart casserole. Spread crumb mixture on top. Bake uncovered for 30-40 minutes until lightly browned. Serve warm or let cool.

Peach Cobbler

Serves 6

1/4 cup margarine, melted
1 cup unbleached all-purpose flour
1 teaspoon baking powder
1/2 teaspoon baking soda
1 cup sugar
1/2 teaspoon salt
1 cup milk (lowfat ok)
1 21-ounce can peach pie filling

Preheat oven to 350°F. Pour margarine in 9x13-inch baking pan, tilting to cover bottom. In mixing bowl, thoroughly combine flour, baking powder, baking soda, sugar and salt. Stir in milk.

Pour batter evenly over melted margarine. Add pie filling evenly on top of batter. Do not stir. Bake for 35-45 minutes until browned. Cool slightly before serving.

Sublime Key Lime

Makes 1 pie

2/3 cup fresh lime juice (key lime when in season)

1 14-ounce can sweetened condensed milk

3 eggs, separated

1 9-inch graham cracker pie crust (see page 124)

6 tablespoons sugar

Preheat oven to 350°F. In food processor or mixer, mix lime juice and condensed milk until smooth. Add egg yolks and blend again. Pour into unbaked pie crust.

To make meringue, beat egg whites until stiff, gradually adding sugar. Spread over pie filling, sealing edges. Bake for 20–25 minutes until top is golden. Cool on wire rack and chill before serving, if desired.

Micro-Wing Custard

Serves 4-6

2 cups milk (lowfat ok)
4 egg yolks
1/2 cup sugar
1/4 teaspoon salt
3 tablespoons cornstarch
2 tablespoons margarine, melted (lowfat ok)
1 teaspoon vanilla
2 squares unsweetened chocolate, melted, optional

Beat milk, egg yolks, sugar, salt and cornstarch. Pour into 2-quart microwave casserole. Microwave on high for 6-7 minutes, stirring with wire whisk after 3 minutes. When cooked, whisk in margarine, vanilla and optional chocolate. Cover. Refrigerate until softly set.

Use remaining egg whites to make meringue cookies (see page 104).

QUICK CHERRY PIE

Cherub Cherry Treat

Serves 6-8

1 cup milk (lowfat ok)

2 eggs

1/2 cup biscuit baking mix

1/4 cup sugar

1/2 teaspoon vanilla extract

2 tablespoons margarine, softened (lowfat ok)

1 21-ounce can cherry pie filling

Preheat oven to 400°F. In large bowl, beat first 6 ingredients for 1 minute. Pour mixture into greased 10-inch pie pan or 11x7-inch baking pan. Spoon pie filling over top. Bake 30-35 minutes until golden brown.

Lemons We Have Curd on High

Makes about 1-1/2 cups

1 cup sugar
4 tablespoons margarine (lowfat ok)
1/3 cup fresh lemon juice
1 tablespoon grated lemon rind
3 eggs, beaten

In non-aluminum saucepan, combine first 4 ingredients. Stir over low heat until sugar dissolves. Pour eggs into hot mixture, stirring constantly. Cook, stirring constantly about 5 minutes until mixture thickens.

Pour into air-tight jar. Refrigerate up to 3 weeks. Use in layer cakes or tarts or on toast.

Rhub-Harp Crisp

Serves 8

1 12-ounce package frozen rhubarb, thawed and drained
1 16-ounce package frozen strawberries or raspberries,
thawed with juice reserved
1/2 cup sugar
2 tablespoons cornstarch

Topping:

1 teaspoon ground cinnamon
1/2 cup uncooked oats
2 tablespoons brown sugar
2 tablespoons oil

Preheat oven to 375°F. Combine rhubarb and berries. In separate bowl, mix 1/3 cup berry juice with sugar and cornstarch. Stir well. Add fruit and mix again. Place in well-greased 8x8-inch baking pan.

In medium bowl, mix together topping ingredients and sprinkle over fruit mixture. Bake for 30 minutes or until topping is lightly browned. Serve warm or let cool.

Heaven Flan Wait

Serves 8

1-1/2 cups sugar
6 eggs, well beaten
1 14-ounce can sweetened condensed milk
2 cups water
1 teaspoon vanilla

Stir sugar in heavy skillet until caramelized, being careful not to burn. Pour over bottom of ungreased, round 2-quart Pyrex dish. Set aside to cool. Mix eggs, sweetened condensed milk, water and vanilla. Pour into caramel-coated dish.

Place filled dish into shallow baking pan filled with one inch of water. Bake at 325°F for 1 hour or until knife inserted in middle comes out clean. Cool 30 minutes then refrigerate. Turn out on plate, caramel side up, before serving.

Michael-an-Gelato

Serves 4-6

4 bananas, peeled and sectioned
2 cups strawberries
Sugar to taste

In blender or food processor, blend bananas and berries. Add sugar to taste. Pour into ice cube trays and freeze. Remove fruit cubes from trays and blend again to make a lowfat, creamy dessert. Serve immediately.

On the other side: Substitute 2 cups of any peeled, seasonal fruit for the berries.

Prayerful Pear-ful

Serves 4

4 large firm pears, peeled
2 tablespoons currants
2 tablespoons chopped walnuts
1/4 cup honey
1 cup regular or non-alcoholic white wine
3 tablespoons red currant or other jelly

Preheat oven to 350°F. Grease a flameproof baking dish large enough to hold pears upright. Core pears, leaving bottoms intact for filling.

In small bowl, combine currants, walnuts and honey. Stuff mixture into each pear. Place pears in prepared baking dish and pour wine over them. Cover with foil. Bake until tender, about 20 minutes.

Remove pears to serving bowl. Place baking dish over medium heat. Add jelly. Cook, stirring until sauce is syrupy, about 7-9 minutes. Pour sauce over warm pears and serve.

Heavenly Hash

Makes 2 pies

2 10-1/2-ounce packages lowfat soft tofu
3/4 cup honey
1/2 cup cocoa powder
3 teaspoons vanilla
1 7-ounce jar marshmallow creme
1/2 cup coarsely chopped pecans or walnuts, optional
2 9-inch no-lard pie crusts, baked, (see page 124)
Lowfat whipped topping, optional

In food processor or blender, whip tofu until smooth. In 2-cup glass measure, heat honey in microwave on medium high for 90 seconds. Pour cocoa into honey, stirring until smooth. Stir in vanilla.

Add chocolate mixture to tofu and blend 1 more minute. Add marshmallow creme and blend just until swirled. Stir in nuts, if desired.

Pour into pie crusts and chill for 1-2 hours. Top with whipped topping, if desired.

Divine Divinity

Makes about 6 dozen

4 cups sugar
1 cup light corn syrup
3/4 cup water
Dash salt
3 egg whites
1 teaspoon vanilla
1/2 cup pecans

Combine sugar corn syrup, water and salt in 2-quart microwave casserole. Microwave on high about 20 minutes, stirring every 5 minutes.

Beat egg whites until very stiff. Pour hot syrup gradually over egg whites, beating at high speed for 10-12 minutes or until thick and candy begins to lose glossy look.

Fold in vanilla and pecans. Drop by small spoonfuls onto wax paper. Let cool.

Best if made on a dry day.

Manna From Heaven

Temptation Tomato Bread

Just Call Me Angel of the Cornbread

Bellini Zucchini

Throne Scones

Our Daily Soda Bread

Heaven Leavened

Manna Banana

Joyful All Ye Muffins Rise

Dominus Vo-Biscuits

Trumpet Crumpets

Temptation Tomato Bread

Makes 1 loaf

3 cups unbleached all-purpose flour

1-1/2 teaspoons baking powder

1 teaspoon baking soda

1/2 teaspoon salt

1 cup grated Parmesan cheese

1 egg, beaten

1/4 cup oil

2 tablespoons honey

3 tablespoons minced fresh parsley or cilantro

3 tablespoons minced fresh or 2 teaspoons dried basil

1 14-ounce can plum tomatoes with liquid, crushed

Poppy seeds for topping

Preheat oven to 350°F. Combine first 5 ingredients in mixing bowl. In separate bowl, combine egg, oil, honey, parsley or cilantro, basil and tomatoes.

Pour wet mixture into dry and stir until blended. Pour batter into a greased 9x5-inch loaf pan. Sprinkle poppy seeds over top. Bake for 40-50 minutes until toothpick or fork inserted in center comes out clean.

Just Call Me Angel of the Cornbread

Serves 8-12

1-1/2 cups yellow cornmeal
1/2 cup unbleached all-purpose flour
1/2 teaspoon salt
Cumin, chili powder and/or cayenne pepper to taste
2 teaspoons baking powder
3 tablespoons margarine, melted
2 tablespoons honey
2 eggs
1-1/2 cups buttermilk or plain yogurt
1 cup shredded cheddar cheese (lowfat ok)

Options:

Sliced green chilies, diced jalapeños, sweet red peppers, minced onions

Preheat oven to 400°F. Combine dry ingredients in medium bowl. In blender or food processor, blend liquid ingredients until creamy. Stir in cheese and optional ingredients.

Mix wet and dry mixtures. Do not overmix. Pour into a greased 8x8-inch baking pan. Bake for 35-40 minutes. Cool on wire rack.

Bellini Zucchini

Makes 2 loaves

3 cups unbleached all-purpose flour

1 teaspoon baking soda

1/2 teaspoon baking powder

1 teaspoon nutmeg

2 teaspoons cinnamon

1 teaspoon salt

2 cups brown sugar, packed

2 cups finely shredded zucchini

3 eggs

1 cup applesauce

1 teaspoon vanilla

1 cup chopped walnuts

1 20-ounce can crushed pineapple, drained

Preheat oven to 350°F. Mix first 7 ingredients in large bowl. In separate bowl, beat zucchini, eggs, applesauce and vanilla until creamy. Mix wet and dry ingredients thoroughly. Fold in nuts and pineapple.

Pour batter into 2 greased 9x5-inch loaf pans. Bake for 60-70 minutes. Bread is done when toothpick or fork inserted in center comes out clean. Cool in pan for 10 minutes, remove and cool thoroughly on wire rack.

Throne Scones

Makes 12

3 cups unbleached all-purpose flour
2 teaspoons baking powder
2 teaspoons baking soda
1/2 teaspoon salt
6 tablespoons cold margarine
2 tablespoons brown sugar, packed
1-1/4 cups plain lowfat yogurt
2 eggs
1/2 cup raisins or currants

Preheat oven to 400°F. Sift together the first 4 ingredients. With food processor or pastry cutter, cut dry mixture together with margarine and brown sugar until uniformly blended. If food processor was used, transfer mixture to a bowl.

Beat yogurt and 1 egg. Pour into pastry mixture. Add fruit and stir just until mixed. Drop by rounded 1/4-cup measures onto greased baking sheet.

Beat remaining egg and brush or pat onto tops of scones. Bake for 12-15 minutes. Serve warm.

Our Daily Soda Bread

Makes one round loaf

3/4 cup raisins

1 cup boiling water

2-3 cups unbleached all-purpose flour

1-1/2 teaspoons baking powder

1/2 teaspoon salt

1/4 teaspoon baking soda

1 cup buttermilk

3 tablespoons honey

1 tablespoon caraway seeds

Preheat oven to 350°F. Cover raisins with boiling water for 10 minutes, then drain and set aside. In large bowl, mix together 2 cups flour, baking powder, salt and baking soda.

In separate bowl, blend buttermilk and honey. Stir in drained raisins and caraway seeds. Add wet mixture into flour mixture a little at a time, mixing to make a soft, slightly sticky dough. If too sticky, add small amount of flour.

Knead for 1 minute. Form into ball and place on greased baking sheet. Slash top with knife. Bake for 40-50 minutes.

Heaven Leavened

Makes 2 loaves

2 packages active dry yeast
2-1/2 cups warm water (105-115°F)
4 tablespoons honey
4 tablespoons margarine, softened
2 teaspoons salt
4 teaspoons total dried dill and/or basil
6 cups unbleached all-purpose flour

In large mixing bowl, dissolve yeast in water. Stir in honey. Add margarine, salt, dill or basil and 4 cups flour. Beat on low speed until blended, then on high speed for 2 minutes. Stir in remaining flour with wooden spoon. Cover and let rise in warm place until doubled, about 45 minutes.

Grease 2 9x5-inch loaf pans. Stir batter 30 strokes with wooden spoon. Place equal amounts into loaf pans. Cover and let rise in warm place about 30 minutes until batter rises to edge of pan.

Bake at 375°F for 35-40 minutes. Remove from pan and cool on wire rack.

Manna Banana

Makes 2 loaves

6 ripe bananas, peeled

1/2 cup applesauce

2 eggs

1-1/2 cups sugar or 1 cup honey

1 teaspoon baking soda

1 teaspoon salt

4 cups unbleached all-purpose flour

1 cup chopped Macadamia or other nuts, optional

Preheat oven to 325°F. Grease 2 9x5-inch loaf pans. In large mixing bowl, beat first 3 ingredients. Slowly blend in sugar or honey. In separate bowl, combine baking soda, salt and flour. Mix wet and dry ingredients.

Stir in nuts if desired. Pour even amounts into loaf pans. Bake for 40-50 minutes until toothpick or fork inserted in center comes out clean.

Joyful All Ye Muffins Rise

Makes 24 muffins

2 cups unbleached all-purpose flour

2 cups sugar

2 teaspoons baking soda

1 teaspoon nutmeg

2 teaspoons cinnamon

1 teaspoon salt

1 16-ounce can pumpkin

4 eggs

1 cup applesauce

1/3 cup water

1 teaspoon vanilla

1 cup chopped pecans or walnuts

1 cup raisins

Preheat oven to 350°F. Mix first 6 ingredients in large bowl. In separate bowl, beat pumpkin, eggs, applesauce, water and vanilla. Mix wet and dry ingredients. Stir in nuts and raisins.

Fill each muffin cup 2/3 full. Bake for 25-30 minutes. Cool in pan for 10 minutes. Remove and cool thoroughly on wire rack.

Dominus Vo-Biscuits

Makes 15-18 biscuits

2 cups unbleached all-purpose flour

2 teaspoons baking powder

1/2 teaspoon salt

1/2 teaspoon baking soda

1/2 cup lowfat plain yogurt

1/4 cup margarine, melted

1 cup finely grated Parmesan cheese

1 egg

2 tablespoons honey

1 tablespoon dried basil

1/4 teaspoon ground black pepper

Mix first four ingredients in large mixing bowl. In separate bowl, beat yogurt, margarine, 3/4 cup Parmesan, egg and honey until frothy. Add basil and pepper and beat again.

Add wet mixture to dry. Mix with spoon until dough holds together. Knead for a few minutes until smooth.

Preheat oven to 425°F. With greased hands, form dough into smooth balls about 1-1/2 inches in diameter. Flatten slightly and place on a baking sheet. Sprinkle tops lightly with remaining Parmesan. Bake for 15 minutes until lightly browned.

Trumpet Crumpets

Makes 8 crumpets

1 package active dry yeast
1 cup warm water
1-2/3 cups scalded milk (lowfat ok)
2 teaspoons sugar
1 teaspoon salt
4 cups unbleached all-purpose flour, sifted
3 tablespoons margarine, softened
8 metal crumpet or English muffin rings*

Dissolve yeast in 2 tablespoons warm water and let stand for 3-5 minutes. Combine milk, remaining water, sugar and salt in mixing bowl. Add yeast mixture and beat in 2 cups flour. Cover and let rise 1-1/2 hours until risen and collapsed back into bowl.

Beat in margarine and remaining flour. Grease insides of rings, place on greased baking sheet and fill half full with batter. Let rise until double. Bake at 425°F for 30-40 minutes until brown.

*Available at gourmet kitchen shops.

INDEX

D

N-O

P-Q

W-Z